Di
The 1906 San Francisco Earthquake and Fire

By Howard Brinkley

BookCaps™ Study Guides
www.bookcaps.com

© 2012. All Rights Reserved.

Table of Contents

ABOUT HISTORYCAPS 3

INTRODCUTION 4

PART 1: THE EARTHQUAKE 7

    LIFE ON A FAULT LINE 8
    RATTLES AND RUPTURES 11
    DESTRUCTION BY THE BAY 14
    THE MAYOR AND THE GENERAL 19

PART 2: THE FIRE 23

    AN 'IMPOSSIBLE' SITUATION 24
    SMALL FIRES MERGE AND SPREAD 26
    FLEEING AND FIGHTING THE FIRES 28
    THE CHIEF'S WARNINGS 35

PART 3: THE AFTERMATH 38

    IN THE RAIN 39
    MEN IN UNIFORM 41
    AN UNPRECEDENTED RELIEF EFFORT 43
    SEPARATE BUT UNEQUAL IN THE CITY 47

PART 4: REBUILDING THE CITY 49

    REBUILDING THE CITY 50
    JUST A LITTLE SHAKE 53
    PHOENIX SPIRIT 56

CONCLUSION 60

    THE LEGACY OF THE DISASTER 61

PHOTOS 63

BIBLIOGRAPHY 67

About HistoryCaps

HistoryCaps is an imprint of BookCaps™ Study Guides. With each book, a brief period of history is recapped. We publish a wide array of topics (from baseball and music to science and philosophy), so check our growing catalogue regularly (**www.bookcaps.com**) to see our newest books.

12th EXTRA — The Seattle Daily Times

SPECIAL MAIL EDITION FOR FRIDAY MORNING, APRIL 20, 1906.

CITY WIPED OUT!
Fire Still Raging!

EYE WITNESS DESCRIBES HORROR!

BEG FOOD FROM SEATTLE!

Introdcution

For modern viewers, the photographs taken in San Francisco on April 18, 1906, call to mind London during the Blitz bombings, or New York City on 9/11. Roofs and chimneys crumble; a menacing haze of dust fills the air; people stand in shock.

But in the City by the Bay, the nightmare came, not from airplanes in the skies but from below. Just after 5 am a massive earthquake hit California, centered under the Pacific Ocean just southwest of San Francisco. People felt it as far north as Oregon and as far south as Los Angeles -- and there were even reports of tremors in central Nevada to the east. But in San Francisco, the earthquake was an unmitigated disaster, beginning with the first shudders and continuing in a horrific fire that burned for three days and nights.

The temblor and resulting fire constituted one of the worst peacetime calamities in American history. While the official San Francisco death toll at the time was about 500, later researchers found the number to be more than 3,000.

Seismically, 1906 was an *annus horribilis*. By April, the year had already included the massive Ecuadorian-Colombian Earthquake, possibly as high as 8.4 on the Richter Magnitude Scale; and a later temblor that killed more than a thousand people in Taiwan.

Then came San Francisco's 1906 earthquake, still the largest recorded in the San Francisco Bay Area. It was 7.7 to 7.9 on the Richter scale; in contrast, the neighboring 1989 Loma Prieta earthquake measured 7.0 and killed fewer than 100 people -- though it did dramatically knock down a section of the Bay Bridge between San Francisco and Oakland.

Part 1: The Earthquake

Life On a Fault Line

San Francisco residents are accustomed to the occasional shudders and jiggles that come with living above the San Andreas Fault. Many are so minor that a person might miss them if he were riding in a newfangled horseless carriage, or sometimes even he were just strolling along the cobblestones.

Earthquakes were also not well understood at the beginning of 1906. The first seismographs in the United States had been installed only 20 years before, in 1887 at the Lick Observatory and the University of California at Berkeley, according to the U.S. Geological Survey's website. Japan and Europe were more advanced, but even so, the theory of plate tectonics did not yet exist. Even geologists had little understanding of how and why earthquakes happened, or of what destruction they could wreak on the United States' West Coast.

And it is easy to get complacent about life on a fault line when it can be years in between big ones. When the weather is mild, and the scenery picturesque and everyone seems to want to live in the Bay Area, with its successful businesses, easy pace of life, dreamy drives and cultural nights out in the city.

Even at the turn of the 20th century, not that long after several ruinous fires had raced through San Francisco during the Gold Rush, many San Franciscans remained unworried about natural disasters. It was a badge of honor to have lived through one.

"Some inhabitants had rebuilt four or five times," journalist Philip L. Fradkin wrote in his 2005 book *The Great Earthquake and Firestorms of 1906*.

"One such landowner was William Rabe ... When Rabe rebuilt for the last time, he had the words *Nil Desperandum* (Never despair) carved in large letters on the façade of his house. He was flattered when people called him by that name. The structure was destroyed in the 1906 fire."

Complacency, too, was knocked flat by the quake. People out for a stroll were thrown onto their faces in the street. Sleepers woke feeling like a giant hand was angrily agitating their homes. Some were jolted plumb out of bed. Indeed, since the hour was early on a Wednesday (5:12 or 5:13 am; accounts differ), most San Franciscans were in bed. This was one of the remarkably few pieces of good news that the city had that morning.

"If the seismic disturbance had occurred in the daytime when the busy thoroughfares of the metropolis were lined with people, or in the evening when the theatres were crowded, there would have been a still more horrifying chapter in the world's history than the one which the city by the Golden Gate has just contributed," a writer penned later that spring in *Organized Labor*, a California union newsletter.

Rattles and Ruptures

There was little time to be thankful on April 18. "The awful call came without warning like a mysterious bolt of lightning," the union author wrote, adding: "In a few seconds the streets in the residence districts were lined with people who rushed out of their apartments and homes in night attire. Furniture, pianos, book cases danced through the rooms as if possessed with demons; crockery and china were dashed out of their snug closets on the floors."

According to the U.S. Geological Survey, the disaster began with a foreshock at 5:12 am, and the main temblor hit 20 to 25 seconds later, lasting almost a minute. The quake ruptured nearly 300 miles of the San Andreas Fault, as compared to the 25-mile rupture caused by the 1989 Loma Prieta quake.

For their years of living near the San Andreas Fault, few San Franciscans had ever felt an earthquake like this. The most recent significant quake had occurred along the neighboring Southern Hayward fault nearly 40 years before. And, no one gets used to the sight of the ground rippling in waves.

Even the aftershocks that came after the main temblors did damage. Running to breakfast at his home in a quiet, sparsely populated neighborhood on the west side of the city, a 4-year-old boy named Ansel Adams was knocked to the ground by an aftershock, geologist Simon Winchester wrote in his 2005 book *A Crack in the Edge of the World.* The youngster who was later to become a famous photographer fell against a brick garden wall and broke his nose.

"His famously chiseled profile was created in that instant," Winchester wrote.

People, of course, were not the only things shaken when the earth moved. The ground ripped open and closed, crushing any object or animal that had the misfortune to fall into the chasm. Country roads got new kinks in them, and urban streets split wide open. In his 2001 book *Disaster!* journalist Dan Kurzman wrote that the seismic wave "was like a rampaging super army."

South of San Francisco, the earthquake turned much of the Stanford University campus to rubble. The spire fell from the top of the elegant Stanford Memorial Church into the chancel, and the university was shut down. Farther south, more than 100 mental patients were killed at the Agnews State Hospital near San Jose when an unreinforced masonry building crumbled. Rescuers dug for days, sometimes bringing forth grateful people, sometimes carrying out corpses. Still farther south in Santa Cruz, the San Lorenzo River bubbled and swirled, then dropped far below its usual level.

And up north in Sonoma County, the picturesque market town of Santa Rosa was hit painfully hard; some said the shaking was worse there than in San Francisco. An estimated 79 people were killed, many of them in large hotels that were destroyed.

A hundred years later, in 2006, residents were still honoring the Santa Rosa dead. On that April 18, a horse-drawn hearse led a mock funeral procession, and firefighters pulled a hand-drawn hose cart, according to the *San Francisco Chronicle*. The city held a safety fair that weekend to educate residents about earthquake preparedness.

Destruction By the Bay

But despite the far-reaching devastation of the 1906 temblor, San Francisco, with its 400,000 residents, panoramic ocean and bay views, spicy red-light Barbary Coast district, and penchant for West Coast romanticism and bohemian spirit, became the poster child for the disaster. And the walls did come tumbling down.

Among the areas hardest hit were the poorer quarters south of Market Street, where ramshackle row houses had been built with shoddy materials and methods, and tended to tumble easily. Brick houses, which also abounded in the city, suffered. They had an air of indestructibility and permanence, but an unreinforced brick building is no match for a 7.7 earthquake. Numerous witnesses described the brick dust hanging in the air after the temblor.

The shaking was also notably rough in the sections of the city built atop "filled" ground that had once been swampland or water. For years, people had been building atop this "made" land, often with remarkably little regard for the consequences. But in a massive earthquake, this type of land seems almost to revert to the area's former state, swaying and almost liquefying.

Mansions in wealthy areas such as Nob Hill, built with strong foundations, weathered the quake. The millionaires who had them constructed, including Leland Stanford, Mark Hopkins and Charles Crocker, could well afford the best materials and craftsmen. But elegant City Hall, $6 million in the making and once gleaming with columns and cornices, looked like a war zone.

"The City Hall is a complete wreck," wrote the *San Francisco Daily News*, the only daily paper in the city to get an edition out on April 18, 1906. "The walls surrounding the grand dome have fallen, leaving only the skeleton frame work and the top of the dome intact," the *Daily News* wrote in a story first printed on pink paper (which may have been the only type available). "Around all sides of the building the walls have crumbled, like so many cards."

Later reports criticized the building's design and workmanship, as well as many of its materials. The brick walls, it was said, were laid in lime mortar of terrible quality, and the fancy architectural ornaments did not have adequate bracing. Some areas had no mortar at all. One of the iconic images of the earthquake is the wretched City Hall, cracked and crumbling, its steel skeleton exposed.

As for San Francisco's other daily newspaper, the *Chronicle*, *Examiner* and *Call* lost their newsrooms to fire, and journalists fled across the bay to put out a highly unusual joint edition with the help of the surviving *Oakland Tribune*. While the enterprising spirit was admirable, the emergency edition contained a significant factual error: It reported that the city was under martial law, which never happened during the disaster.

For the Friday paper, the standard competition resumed among the reporters. The *Examiner* wrangled sole use of the *Tribune*'s printing plant, and journalists from the *Call* and *Chronicle* had to scramble to make other arrangements in the East Bay, Fradkin wrote: "The united effort had lasted only one night."

Meanwhile, a list of other prominent San Francisco structures cut down by the quake reads like a Who's Who of buildings: the Academy of Sciences, the Aetna Building, the Majestic Theater. The Central Emergency Hospital turned from a haven into a debris-filled nightmare, and the four-story Valencia Street Hotel, a bustling boarding house, sank up to its third floor, with horrendous consequences. "Scores of people on the first two floors drowned in water flooding in from a broken water main in front of the hotel, many of them apparently after lingering in agony," Kurzman wrote.

Interestingly, the U.S. Mint building, nicknamed the Granite Lady, was solidly built and weathered the quake. But that was no promise of posterity.

"The building, its massive blocks fire-singed, remains standing today on the 500 block of Mission Street," Winchester wrote. "But it is empty and unused, because the city of San Francisco cannot afford to bring it up to today's earthquake-proof standards."

Beyond destroying individual buildings, the earthquake also wreaked considerable havoc on systems that connected homes together -- and connected them with crucial resources. Like the mighty redwood trees that fell north of the city, utility poles toppled, leaving electrical wires to arc in the streets in the company of broken glass and splintered wood. Telegraph wires broke, cutting off communications and silencing the previously incessant clicks of the telegraph offices. Gas pipes cracked, leaked and broke. And, all over the city, cast-iron water pipes and cisterns suffered serious fractures. Right away, people noticed that their faucets had suddenly stopped working.

Before long, it would become abundantly and tragically clear that the fire hydrants were just as dry.

The Daily News' headline for April 18 foreshadows the tragedies yet to come: "HUNDREDS DEAD! Fire Follows Earthquake, Laying Downtown Section in Ruins -- City Seems Doomed For Lack of Water."

The Mayor and the General

As the disaster unfolded, two decidedly different men would take charge in San Francisco. Mayor Eugene Schmitz, a tall man with a black beard and a background as a violinist and an orchestra conductor, was dogged by allegations of corruption. He had some uncommonly powerful friends, including William Randolph Hearst, who was not a bad guy to know when newspaper endorsements were on the line. Still, in the days before the earthquake hit, a corruption investigation was drawing ever closer to the mayor, fueled by the money of sugar baron Rudolph Spreckels.

Also, powerful in the City by the Bay was the robust Brigadier General Frederick Funston, deputy commander of the U.S. Army garrison in the Presidio in the northern part of San Francisco. He was war-scarred and the proud owner of a Congressional Medal of Honor that he had earned fighting rebels in the Philippines. Ordinarily, he would have been second-in-command of the army soldiers in San Francisco, but on April 18 his superior, Major General Adolphus Greely, was out of town.

Both men were awakened in their beds at home by the earthquake, Funston on Nob Hill and Schmitz west of downtown. Both dressed and hurried outside.

Funston headed for the army headquarters in the Phelan Building a few blocks away to direct rescue operations, but the structure was heavily damaged and empty, Kurzman wrote. Before long, Funston saw the fires beginning and the firefighters struggling with dry hydrants. He foresaw a splendid blaze coming, in which the army would be sorely needed to protect the people and public and private property. "Funston now saw fit to order all available troops into the city; in effect, to institute martial law on his own, though this was illegal," Kurzman wrote. Not a fan of Mayor Schmitz, he ordered in the troops on his own.

Though martial law was never declared, by noon on April 18 Funston had more than 1,500 soldiers in the city, according to Kurzman. Before long he had wired U.S. Secretary of War Taft for rations and tents for 20,000 people, saying, "I shall do everything in my power to render assistance and trust to the War Department to authorize any action I may have to take." Funston was rapidly becoming, as Kurzman put it, "the military dictator of a fascist-style San Francisco."

As for Schmitz, he quickly learned that City Hall had been wrecked, and made his way toward it in an aide's car. Along the way, he was stunned to learn that Funston had ordered in the troops without consulting him, Kurzman wrote.

Schmitz swiftly headed for the basement of the Hall of Justice and set up a temporary city hall there by candlelight -- the electricity was gone -- to make a plan to save the city. "If Funston took immediate charge, Mayor Schmitz promptly joined him in equal stature," Winchester wrote. Schmitz issued orders to have soldiers cordon off burning areas, keep gawkers away, and secure the Treasury. He instituted a nighttime curfew, and ordered gas and electrical companies to suspend services for the time being. The city remained dark for several days, except for the macabre glow of the fires.

Schmitz's controversial order remains vivid to this day and is quoted in many history books: "The Federal Troops, the members of the Regular Police Force and all Special Police Offices have been authorized by me to KILL any and all persons engaged in Looting or in the Commission of Any Other Crime."

Schmitz also formed the Committee of Fifty, a band of leading city residents, as a ruling circle. These were not working-class men; they included Spreckels and James D. Phelan, one of the wealthiest men in the city, a former mayor and an avid reformer. One may well wonder about Schmitz's ulterior motives in choosing several of the men who had been leading an anticorruption effort against him.

However, Schmitz may have felt about having federal troops in his city, he must have realized that even the enhanced force was not enough to maintain order as the fires grew. He asked Funston for more troops, contacted California Governor George Pardee to call in the National Guard, and later wired a U.S. naval station these words: "Earthquake, town on fire, send marines and tugs."

The Committee of Fifty's first meeting was abruptly interrupted when the wind shifted, and the fire moved toward the Hall of Justice. They fled to Nob Hill to attempt to resume the meeting in the Fairmont Hotel.

The committee would be forced to move twice more the next day as the flames kept spreading.

Part 2: The Fire

An 'Impossible' Situation

How could a city that was on the tip of a peninsula, with water on three sides burn? Walk far enough in three out of four directions in this compact city and you will eventually end up either in San Francisco Bay or the Pacific Ocean. And yet with water everywhere, there was barely enough to fight a fire on the scale of the 1906 inferno.

Only seconds after the earthquake's shudders and rolls subsided, the city was already burning in countless places. Before the blazes were through, they spread over 490 city blocks. And they were probably unstoppable.

The situation, Winchester wrote, "was made impossible because of the sheer number of fires that erupted all across the city almost simultaneously. No fire department anywhere in America, or possibly anywhere in the world, could have possibly dealt properly with this conflagration, had they all the water that they could use. The 1906 fire was essentially uncontrollable, somewhat akin to the firestorms that ruined Dresden and Tokyo, and that raged in the aftermath of the atomic bombing of Hiroshima."

What started all these fires? Everything began with the earthquake. A city lit mainly by gas lighting and heated mostly by coal and wood stoves was highly vulnerable to shaking. When the chimneys fell, the stoves rattled and toppled, the coal oil lamps tipped over and the gas pipes broke, flames erupted. Whether a street's calamity was a fallen power line meeting a shattered gas pipe or a shower of fireplace embers hitting a wooden roof, the result was the same.

The official report by the San Francisco Fire Department in 1907 read in part: "It is positively known that there were over fifty fires in different locations at one time that morning, and probably there were many more that were put out by the occupants of the houses where they occurred."

In many cases, people who had been trapped in the rubble of falling buildings after the quake now faced the horror of being burned alive. Anecdotes abound of victims realizing they were trapped and begging passing policemen to shoot them.

Small Fires Merge and Spread

Some fires will never have their stories told; others became legendary. South of Market Street, the earthquake knocked over heating fires in a laundry business, starting what became called the Chinese Laundry Fire. In central San Francisco, in the now-trendy neighborhood of Hayes Valley, a woman reportedly decided to make breakfast in her building that had seemed only barely wounded by the quake. Unfortunately, so the story goes, she did not realize that her chimney had been damaged.

The resulting blaze, one of the worst of the day, came to be known as the Ham and Eggs Fire. Its fallout included the loss of much of Hayes Valley and the nearby Mission District.

"Had there been the slightest quantity of water obtainable when this … fire was discovered it could have easily been extinguished, but we were compelled to watch it burn and spread," a fire-department official wrote in the department's report.

Unlike the poor Hayes Valley woman, other people who started fires after the earthquake reportedly did so on purpose. Fire damage was commonly covered by insurance policies. Earthquake damage (an "Act of God") rarely was, if at all.

Fires are social beings, and once the 50 or more blazes began in the city they were ready to combine forces. The windy weather helped them to meet, and the clear spring sky offered no meteorological assistance in putting them out. The blazes continued to spread, leveling neighborhoods and continuing to others that still had flammable materials: parlor pianos, carpets, rocking chairs, barrels; books, artwork, photographs and civic records that could never be replaced. What was worse, once the fires merged, they formed their own air currents.

"They began to suck more and more oxygen from the atmosphere and to create winds of their own, eddies of superheated air that sucked ever more of the islands of fire together," Winchester wrote. "By midday, there was a wall of flame a mile and a half long to the south of Market Street, and the wall of smoke rose at least two miles up into the sky, visible across all the counties of the bay and horrifying thousands."

Fleeing and Fighting the Fires

By this time, the people who could flee were doing so, in every direction they could. With the fires raging in the northeast quadrant of the city, which was most heavily populated and built-up, refugees fled west to Golden Gate Park or south toward the Peninsula. Today's Sunset District out by the Pacific Ocean was then still mostly dunes, and also offered refuge. Other people looked for safety across the bay, bolting toward San Francisco's Ferry Building in hopes of boarding a boat to Oakland.

Countless reported memories summon up vivid images of the refugees dragging trunks or wagons with whatever they could rescue, pressing handkerchiefs to their faces, dodging embers and cinders and falling rubble, bulky in several layers of rescued clothing, carrying terrified children and pets. There are many anecdotes of refugees toting their parrots or other feathered pets in cages, and one pet store reportedly handed out its birds to passers-by rather than letting the animals perish in the flames. At least one person fled carrying a goldfish in a full bowl.

Emma M. Burke, who took refuge in the park and later wrote about her recollections for *Overlook Magazine* in an article that has been reprinted in many places, recalled fleeing in a heavy wool skirt and long coat, her cash and diamonds secreted inside a hand satchel.

"The immense fires started by the earthquake now made such a ruddy glow that it was easy to see everything, although the flames were two miles away. No lights were allowed in the Park, and all was soon quiet except the wail of a baby, the clang of an ambulance, and the incessant roll of wheels and tramp of feet," she wrote. "People were all about us in huddled groups, sleeping the sleep of exhaustion on the lawns and under the shrubbery."

While the quake had hit the poor with a more vicious blow, the fire did not discriminate. Rather than remaining in the crowded areas south of Market Street, or simply burning the Chinatown ghetto and the flophouses of the Barbary Coast, it moved ever forward, ultimately consuming the mansions on Nob Hill where many of the wealthy had stood and watched the spectacle below. Burned, too, were the expensive houses made from California redwood, the Grand Opera House, the Call and Examiner newspaper buildings.

Even the Palace Hotel, made of brick and iron, patrolled by watchmen and furnished in Louis XV style, was not immune. The Palace had a dedicated water supply of its own and thousands of feet of fire hose, and that was not enough to save it. Some had billed the Palace as fireproof; six years later, an equally grand little boat would be billed as unsinkable.

In the overleaf of his book, Fradkin traces the spread of the firestorm with the help of a map. The first day, the fire engulfed the areas around Market Street: south of Market, City Hall and the Mechanics' Pavilion, the Produce District just north of Market. On the second day, the flames headed west and ravaged the Mission District, including the house of James D. Phelan. On this day, the fire also traveled north to swallow posh Nob Hill, as well as the Fairmont Hotel, where the Committee of Fifty had been meeting.

On the third day, the crowded, cramped Chinatown ghetto burned. So did Telegraph Hill and the traditional Italian neighborhood of North Beach, both places where most of the houses were made of redwood and pine. On its march north, the fire was stopped only by the bay.

The fire department did what it could. At the time, according to the fire department's report, the force had 584 men in uniform, 38 steam fire engines, 10 hook-and-ladder companies, and 50 handheld chemical extinguishers. Much of this equipment did exceptionally little good when only drips were coming out of the fire hydrants. It was determined later that the reservoirs serving San Francisco had not been harmed by the earthquake but that all of the conduits from the reservoirs had been damaged, leaving no way to pipe in the 80 million gallons that would have done wonders against the fire. Pipes were cracked, thrown to one side. In at least one case, as was reported from the conduit that led from Crystal Springs Dam, an iron pipeline was thrown into the air and then landed on top of its wooden trestle, splintering it.

The result: useless coils of hose in the streets, people screaming for water, and trained firefighters standing helplessly by, with no working telephones or fire-alarm systems to help them communicate. Only a supremely few hydrants dispensed water, in some cases salt water from the ocean.

People grabbed any liquid they could find to try to staunch the flames. In his book, Fradkin compiled a partial list: barrels of wine and vinegar, sewer water, water from burst mains, well water, and even soda water from siphons. Other reports described people using bottles of juice, throwing horse blankets over piles of embers and gathering water from lily ponds and rain barrels.

The most dramatic and controversial means of attempting to slow the fire's spread was the use of dynamite. At one point, the once-bustling Van Ness Avenue, a dividing line between the eastern and western parts of the city, became a fire line. Mayor Schmitz and General Funston agreed that "blowing up buildings on or near Van Ness was the only way to stop the fire before it burst into the western part of the city," Kurzman wrote. But which buildings, and where?

Schmitz advocated blowing up only the structures just ahead of the fire "because they were doomed anyway and also because he would save the homes of his rich, important colleagues," Kurzman wrote. Funston wanted to dynamite the buildings much farther ahead, "in order to create a wasteland too vast for the flames to hurdle." The mayor won.

But in many cases, people reported that improper use of dynamite ended up spreading the fire farther. Oftentimes, the explosives were set off by firefighters who had never used them before. The naval officers from Mare Island who arrived later were more schooled in the practice. Meanwhile, though, the booms terrified residents and animals who were already shell-shocked, and often did no good.

In some places, dynamite was set off too close to unburned buildings. At Van Ness, the explosions made fiery rubble fly to other blocks, where new fires started. In some instances, people begged the soldiers not to blow up their homes, to no avail.

Ultimately, the mayor changed his mind and sided with Funston's plan, hoping to create a gap of downed buildings that the fires could not jump. "Schmitz would write off the whole part of the city east of Van Ness and throw everything into the battle along that superwide avenue," Kurzman wrote.

More dynamite was late in coming, and several fires started on the west side of the avenue, including one in the St. Mary's Cathedral steeple, Kurzman wrote. Two priests climbed up and tore away the burning parts of the roof with an axe, and the church was saved. When the dynamite arrived, along with a blessed but small flow of water from a few hoses, men fought the fire just west of Van Ness throughout the night of April 19 and into the morning. The fire finally died out -- until someone dynamited another building on Van Ness and the district went up again.

Overall, the fires burned for three days. "They eventually burned themselves out on Saturday, and only after everything flammable had been consumed," Winchester wrote.

And then it rained.

More than 28,000 buildings had been destroyed, including schools, libraries, firehouses, emergency hospitals and the county jail. Some 200,000 people were now homeless.

The Chief's Warnings

San Francisco had a history of fires, many of them erupting in the unruly days of the Gold Rush just a half-century before. So many people had warned of the continuing fire danger before 1906. One of the most prominent cautioners was silenced just before the exact disaster he had predicted came true.

San Francisco Fire Chief Dennis Sullivan had been warning the municipal government for 13 years -- his tenure as chief -- that he needed more funds to protect the city, Kurzman wrote. He was concerned about the quality of the 25-year-old subterranean cisterns that stored the water his men would need if the water mains broke in an earthquake. He advocated for the purchase of a fireboat, which the department did not have.

"Sullivan had drawn up an intricate plan to reactivate the cisterns, acquire firefighting equipment, build a supplementary saltwater system, house high explosives, and train his men to use them in checking fires. He had long foreseen what would happen if a fire raced out of control, especially after an earthquake, and threatened to ravage the city," Kurzman wrote.

The chief found support for his ideas in the National Board of Fire Underwriters, who concurred in an October 1905 report that "the potential hazard is very severe," Kurzman wrote. The report went on to mention "the almost total lack of sprinklers and absence of modern protective devices generally, numerous and mutually aggravating conflagration breeders, high winds, and comparatively narrow streets" in San Francisco. Mayor Schmitz, though, preferred to direct funding toward the railroads, the water and light companies, and other firms. It was only just before the earthquake that he had finally agreed to create a citizens' committee to study the needs of Sullivan's 55 fire stations. Sullivan was scheduled to testify in front of the committee on April 18, and was said to be eagerly awaiting the opportunity to plead his case.

But a few hours before that appointment, the earthquake hit. Next door to the fire station where Sullivan and his wife, Margaret, were sleeping, the top of the California Hotel toppled. It fell onto the fire station, smashing through three floors and into the cellar. The Sullivans plunged as well and were buried by debris, Kurzman wrote. Margaret survived, but the chief died a few days later in the hospital from his injuries, which included dreadful burns from where he had landed on a radiator.

In the early 1920s, a new fire chief's residence was built and named for Sullivan, according to the Museum of the City of San Francisco. To this day, the department chief still lives there, in the company of a bronze tablet with a picture of Sullivan.

Part 3: The Aftermath

In the Rain

When the April showers at last came, they were painful not only because they had waited until after three days of fire. They also added still more misery and discomfort to the hundreds of thousands of homeless San Franciscans, who were living in vacant lots, burned-out buildings, desolate parks, and now-soggy tent cities. Many were wounded, hungry and thirsty. Long lines of people waiting for the sparse supply of water snaked around parks.

Some survivors were able to return to their homes, but this did not always mean luxury. Emma Burke and her husband got back to their "desolated flat" from Golden Gate Park on the fourth night of the disaster, she wrote.

"In the night it poured. The fallen chimneys had torn through the ceilings into two of our rooms; the flat tin roof had thus been bent down, and now acted as a funnel. We heard an ominous drip, drip, and then a steady splash.

"We dared not light a candle -- it was against military orders. So we groped along, hand in hand, through the fallen furniture, pictures, and bundles, and found the water beating a merry tattoo on my sewing-machine, velvet carpet, and some overturned books. ... On account of our inability to cope with the flood that poured in on us, the three flats below us were terribly much damaged by water."

Men In Uniform

The story of men in uniform during the disaster, be they U.S. Army troops, National Guardsmen or policemen, is a checkered one. Besides enforcing curfews and the rules against candles and other flames, the men were busy keeping order, aiding victims and attempting to staunch the fires. They also enlisted many passers-by -- even unwilling civilian men -- to help with whatever was needed: clearing away bulky debris to help rescue people trapped underneath; rounding up escaped, frightened livestock; and stopping looters.

The last category remains one of the most contentious. Did troops "shoot to kill" looters, as the mayor had ordered? Accounts differ to this day.

In Winchester's book, he states that "very few people were actually shot on Schmitz's order," perhaps two, although later he allows that the number is "probably higher" because gunshot wounds are hard to find in bodies burned beyond recognition.

Fradkin's research turned up a number of anecdotes of civilians, innocent or otherwise, being killed by fellow civilians or men in uniform after accusations of looting. In one instance, three men were arrested and tried after allegedly shooting a men driving a Red Cross car, Fradkin wrote. They told the court that they had mistakenly believed martial law was in effect and that looters were using cars. The jury found them not guilty.

General Funston "waffled when he stated that there was no 'well-authenticated case of a single person being killed by regular army troops," but that two men were shot by the state militia, Fradkin wrote. Ultimately, the author concluded that "the exact number, or even an approximate tally, of citizens killed by the military … is unknown."

In some accounts, fire survivors accused the men in uniform themselves of looting food, valuables and other items. On the other hand, there were reports of "benign looting," in which the military allowed kids to help themselves to sweets from the damaged Blum's Candy Store.

An Unprecedented Relief Effort

Feeding the hungry in the wake of the disaster was, in fact, the top priority of the Committee of Fifty, which "took over almost every function of city government," Fradkin wrote. Empty stomachs, the committee decided, "bred unease."

Rabbi Jacob Voorsanger, whose Temple Emanu-El had been destroyed, was the committee member in charge of the food subcommittee. By Friday, he was supervising the dispersal of thousands of loaves of bread, the mayor having decreed that certain bakeries were allowed to operate again under heavy fire regulations.

Meanwhile, huge amounts of relief were pouring in quickly from other cities and states, in the form of funds, food, supplies and household goods. Items in this unprecedented relief effort included army boots, toys, flour, medicines, blankets, biscuits, condensed milk and cured beef. (One well-meaning donation was offered by Philadelphia to undamaged Los Angeles, who declined.)

Big-name men including John D. Rockefeller, Andrew Carnegie and William Randolph Hearst gave thousands of dollars. One figure estimates that almost $10 million (in 1906 dollars) was spent on relief. The Committee of Fifty, the Red Cross, soldiers and citizens worked to disperse the donations in an orderly fashion, dividing the city into relief districts.

"At the same time, Americans were donating to the victims of the eruption of Vesuvius in Italy and a Chilean earthquake. For a short time, it seemed as if the world were falling apart," Fradkin wrote.

During this time, at least half the population of the city of San Francisco was homeless, according to many accounts. Perhaps tens of thousands took shelter in parks, with 2,000 of them camped in Golden Gate Park. Later, the ubiquitous tiny but popular green earthquake cottages, of two or three rooms each, began popping up under the auspices of a city relief committee. They were constructed in the camps and later moved to other locations throughout the city or dismantled. Occupants were charged a nominal rent, and the program was deemed successful.

Before that, though, many San Franciscans left the city, to mixed receptions in other municipalities. Across the bay, Oakland was the most welcoming, setting up its own refugee camps and ultimately providing services to perhaps a fourth of San Francisco's population. Not everyone was happy about the flood of needy, but many of the survivors were helped and some stayed, increasing the smaller city's populace.

Not all cities were so willing to accept refugees. "People wanted to open their hearts, their homes, and their communities, but they were fearful of who they might get -- people with yellow or brown skins, drunkards, criminals, and prostitutes. San Francisco was paying for its reputation -- whether deserved or not -- as a fun-loving, sinful bohemian city," Fradkin wrote.

Some city officials offered help, while others voiced concern about criminal elements, smallpox and general undesirables coming to their area. Salt Lake City offered jobs; Portland, Oregon, provided meals and lodging; San Jose said its jails could take San Francisco's prisoners. Just to the south of San Francisco, though, fearful San Mateo County officials asked the governor for more weapons and ammunition to help keep the peace they thought would be endangered by the refugees.

As the days passed, San Francisco found itself hosting some unwelcome visitors, too. Several publications decried the out-of-towners and casual photographers who came to the city after the disaster to gawk at the ruins, to indulge morbid curiosity and even to plunder.

"The trans-bay ferry boats are crowded, and most of the passengers are those who go to gratify curiosity," a writer chastised in the Berkeley *Reporter*, in an article reprinted on the website of the Museum of the City of San Francisco. "While the stricken ones stand sadly by, dumb with sorrow … the empty hee-haw of vacant minds rings echoing among bare, ghostly walls, as the incongruities of chaos appeal to the small sense of humor possessed by rudimentary brains."

Separate But Unequal In the City

Many reports came from San Francisco refugee camps of people crossing class and race lines in the camps to share what food and goods they had, to gather for prayer and recollection. Some called this "earthquake love" and praised the new feeling of community.

But the Chinese, long discriminated against in San Francisco, remained apart in many cases in the city. Police reportedly segregated them into their own corner of Golden Gate Park. Other populations were treated unequally, as well. "The few Japanese and African Americans melted into the crowds, sought safety by themselves, or fled the city entirely. The poor white refugees who did not seek housing in the official camps received little help," Fradkin wrote.

Relief efforts centered on the northern parts of the city while poorer people south of Market Street were often more in need and had no resources to leave their neighborhoods. In some cases, they were helped by individual donors such as the Mission District's James Rolph, who later became the popular mayor "Sunny Jim." The militant and fearless Father Peter C. Yorke, chancellor to the archbishop, was an ardent supporter of the Irish-Catholic working class.

The Chinese had left their neighborhood by necessity; the tiny, ghetto-like streets and the tenement buildings in them had been annihilated by the fire. Many had settled in Oakland, but thousands roamed San Francisco in search of shelter and work elsewhere. The city formed a committee to "decide where they should be put," Winchester wrote. "No thought was given at first to where the Chinese themselves might want to live"; rather, the committee decided to set up an "Oriental City" in a desolate, distant southeastern part of San Francisco.

The Chinese, though, wanted their old community back, rebuilt in the same spot not far from downtown, Winchester wrote. It took the backing of the Chinese government in Peking to make this possible -- aided by the reminder that this government owned land in the area and planned to rebuild the consulate there. Chinatown remains in the same area, in the heart of the busy northeastern quadrant of the city today, its homes and businesses vibrant.

Part 4: Rebuilding the City

Rebuilding the City

Before the earthquake, the Chicago architect Daniel Hudson Burnham had created a plan to revamp and redesign San Francisco. City notables had turned to him to re-envision their municipality as a cosmopolitan capital of culture and beauty, all remnants of frontier days and wildness and the fisticuffs of the Gold Rush gone. Just one day before the quake, Burnham had delivered a sweeping, extravagant, expensive plan modeled on the grandeur of Paris. There were colonnades, reflecting pools, enormous parks and mansions.

The plans burned with City Hall. So did their ambitions. While San Francisco could have been seen as a clean slate available for artistic experimentation and architectural reinvention, financial worries and the desire to rebuild quickly took priority. "The crying need of San Francisco is not more parks and boulevards; it is business," Michael De Young, one of the founders of the daily Chronicle newspaper, wrote after the cataclysm. Administrators and businessmen wanted to bring the city back to life, and fast. No one had time for fountains and folderol.

"The city center's commercial buildings were hastily put back up, with very few of them either nobly or loftily made, and the houses that were then crowded into their outer boroughs were made less lovely than they might have been, their architectural styles often merely sentimental, nostalgic, or plain faux," Winchester wrote. Visually, San Francisco today is usually praised for its hills, views and Golden Gate Bridge (built in the 1930s) rather than its urban architecture.

Fortunately, though, many of the structures built after the earthquake have proved to be more resilient than their forefathers. After 1906, building features such as steel skeletons and reinforced concrete supports became common, and modern fire stations were constructed -- along with an auxiliary water system. Seismic regulations and building codes were strengthened.

However, many new structures were hastily thrown up before the stricter rules were put in place. And quite a few builders seemed to ignore the lessons of history, regardless of how recent and vivid they were.

In 1915, San Francisco hosted the Panama-Pacific International Exposition world's fair to celebrate both the Panama Canal and the city's recovery from the quake. Most of the gaudy structures were temporary, and that northern piece of the city became today's pricey Marina District.

Unfortunately for the Marina's residents, the neighborhood was built on the same type of "filled" ground that had been so affected by the shaking of the 1906 earthquake. In fact, some of the fill was debris from the '06 temblor.

When the Loma Prieta earthquake hit in 1989, hardly any of the buildings in San Francisco's city center suffered substantial damage, having been built more sturdily than their predecessors. Other buildings, several stretches of freeway and bridge, and the Marina were not so fortunate. "San Francisco's Marina District, with its pretty houses hastily and greedily thrown up on land so unstable that it pulped thixotropically the moment it was shaken (just as the notorious "made-ground" areas of landfill liquefied in 1906), was particularly hard-hit," Winchester wrote.

Again fire broke out and again the water mains cracked. Firefighters had to pump water from the bay to keep the Marina from burning. Newspapers the day after the temblor showed Marina buildings drooping at sickening diagonals, looking a bit like the old Valencia Street Hotel.

Just a Little Shake

Why do people keep building and living in earthquake-prone areas? Some refuse to live in the Bay Area; others take up residence there, but only with well-equipped disaster kits in their homes; and many residents simply do not think much about the risks.

Certainly, if everyone suddenly became terrified of earthquakes and moved away, San Francisco's economy would topple. Many reports in 1906 state that many officials strove after the disaster to minimize San Francisco's reputation as a dangerous, shaky place on the edge of the continent. The official death toll at the time, 498, strikes many researchers today as laughably low.

Gladys Hansen of the Museum of the City of San Francisco, an influential scholar of 1906, puts the death toll at 3,000. Her research has covered cemetery and orphanage records, and interviews with survivors and family members, Kurzman wrote.

"Mayor Schmitz and his political and business cronies not only conspired to fictionalize the death toll, it would appear, but they also falsely minimized the earthquake's role in the catastrophe, attributing most deaths almost all the damage to the fire," Kurzman wrote. "As a result, many desperate homeless, accepting these claims, built new dangerously unstable wood-frame houses, even on 'made' ground. …

"Again, why frighten away investment with tales of natural disaster that only God could control? Fires, on the other hand, could be controlled with better fire-safety measures."

Over and over, a reader researching the 1906 disaster will hear the same refrain about its aftermath: Officials played up the fire and downplayed the quake, some even describing it as minor. Perhaps this was for business reasons; perhaps it was simply easier to think about a catastrophe that could be more easily protected against.

Either way, it is easy to find examples of this phenomenon. The San Francisco Real Estate Board voted on a resolution a week after April 18 that the disaster should always be referred to as the "San Francisco Fire." A railroad official urged California chambers of commerce to tell people that the real enemy had been the fire. Geologists complained of having their data on the earthquake suppressed.

Meanwhile, many insurance companies, hit with a flood of claims, initiated long, dragged-out arguments over whether damages had been caused by the fire or the earthquake, the latter of which would not be covered. "A scant six of the one hundred firms involved were said to have performed impeccably, paying all of their policyholders in full and on time," Winchester wrote. Some companies simply went belly-up.

Phoenix Spirit

Whether San Franciscans in 1906 were insurance agents or city administrators or just plain residents, they often had one thing in common: pride in their home. The City by the Bay has been praised consistently throughout the years for its resilience, optimism and general pluckiness. This may come from being on the edge of the country, balancing on a fault line or from just having that wacky West Coast reputation. San Francisco likes to paint itself as a phoenix. Even on its city seal, where ever since 1859 a phoenix has been depicted rising from the flames.

The 1906 catastrophe did have a few silver linings. When Chinatown was rebuilt, it was no longer the claustrophobia-inducing, warrenlike ghetto it had been. And many buildings in various parts of the city, as has been stated, were rebuilt with stronger, less vulnerable bodies. Some links of friendship were forged between communities. The Calvary Presbyterian Church, for one, gave sanctuary to the Jews who had lost their Temple Emanu-El, prompting Rabbi Voorsanger to write, "We are one people at the present time, and sectarian lines are very faint indeed," as Kurzman quoted him.

Interestingly, the disaster also prompted a leap forward in transportation technology. Beforehand, the automobile had not been a popular beast on the streets of San Francisco. The city was both forward-looking and peculiarly Luddite in some ways, and many denounced the car as a silly toy of the wealthy, a polluting waste that scared horses. But the wheeled conveyance proved to be a godsend after the ground shook, the trains and streetcars would no longer run, and horses dropped dead from exhaustion and smoke inhalation.

"They sped the wounded to the hospitals, carried the dead to the morgues, flashed past with doctors and nurses, city officials, and army officers," Burke wrote of automobiles. "One chauffeur I knew ran his auto for forty-eight hours without rest, resuming after a brief nap to carry dynamite to blown down threatening walls."

For its part, the Chronicle declared the autos "devil wagons turned into chariots of mercy."

Survivors tried to keep their heads and even their humor during the disaster, and some reported moments of levity. Even as the fires raged, men in the streets "met, were introduced, exchanged business cards of places consumed by the flames, appreciated the joke, and went their way," Burke wrote.

An enterprising spirit, too, ultimately saved some of the city's burgeoning businesses, including the small Bank of Italy. Founder Amadeo Peter Giannini, known as A.P., had a reputation for lending to lower-income people who were starting their own fledgling businesses. He was having success among his countrymen, in the Italian neighborhood of North Beach. "So prosperous had the bank become that, in July 1905, it was able to disburse to stockholders more than $5,000, a hefty sum at that time," Kurzman wrote.

On the night before the quake, Giannini went to bed in his home south of San Francisco, in the Peninsula town of San Mateo. His actions the next day, both up in the city and back home, in San Mateo, would become legendary in the banking world.

When the quake hit, Giannini's thoughts focused on keeping his bank safe, but the trains were not running. He covered the 17 miles up the Peninsula to the city running, walking and hitching rides in horse-drawn wagons through the cracked roads packed with debris and hysterical refugees, Kurzman wrote. After five hours, he reached his still-standing bank and its $80,000 worth of gold and silver. With the fire spreading in the city, Giannini made a quick decision to take the assets of his bank home to San Mateo, carrying them in two borrowed produce wagons.

On that now-famous trip back down the Peninsula, the money remained hidden in the wagons under paper records, furniture and crates of orange that gave it a fruity smell for weeks, according to Fradkin. Giannini and his employees drove all night along back roads to hide from thieves, the burning city casting an eerie glow behind them, and the banker hid the fortune in his home fireplace.

After the disaster, Giannini reopened his bank in his brother's Van Ness Avenue home, determined to help his customers rebuild with the help of his loans, Fradkin wrote. He set up a second location "on a plank laid over two barrels on the Washington Street wharf."

"Either one of these temporary locations," Fradkin wrote, "could be considered the future Bank of America's first branch."

Conclusion

The Legacy of the Disaster

From banking to Buicks to building codes, from gallows humor to unspeakable tragedy, the effects and changes engendered by the 1906 earthquake and disaster were far-reaching and long-lasting. Perhaps the catastrophe's most notable legacy was simply this: knowledge.

According to the U.S. Geological Survey, the quake of '06 signified the beginning of modern-day scientific study of California's San Andreas fault system. It was also a crucial turning point for seismic knowledge in the United States, which had long lagged behind Japan and Europe. Scientists all over the Bay Area sprang into action after the quake hit, gathering observations, studying the effects, forming a State Earthquake Investigation Commission.

Published in 1908, the commission's report was "an exhaustive compilation" of seismograph reports of the quake from around the globe; studies of Northern California geography; photos of the damage; and surveys of the earth's movement.

"To this day," a U.S.G.S. report reads, "the report remains a document of the highest regard among seismologists, geologist and engineers -- a benchmark for future, integrated investigations into the effects of earthquakes in the United States."

The effort led to a better understanding of how earthquakes happen, how they might be predicted, and how hazards might be reduced. As the population of the San Francisco Bay Area grows, undoubtedly so will the knowledge.

Photos

S.F. BEFORE THE FIRE

The Call=Chronicle=Examiner

SAN FRANCISCO, THURSDAY, APRIL 19, 1906.

EARTHQUAKE AND FIRE: SAN FRANCISCO IN RUINS

Death and destruction have been the fate of San Francisco. Shaken by a temblor at 5:13 o'clock yesterday morning, the shock lasting 48 seconds, and scourged by flames that raged diametrically in all directions, the city is a mass of smouldering ruins. At six o'clock last evening the flames, seemingly playing with increased vigor, threatened to destroy such sections as their puny had spared during the earlier portion of the day. Building their path in a triangular circuit from the start in the early morning, they jockeyed as the day waned, left the business section, which they had entirely devastated, and skipped in a dozen directions to the residence portions. As night fell they had made their way over into the North Beach section and spreading south to the south they reached out along the shipping section down the Bay shore, over the hills and across toward Third and Townsend streets. Warehouses, wholesale houses and manufacturing concerns fell in their path. Thus completed the destruction of the entire district known as the "South of Market Street." How far they are reaching to the south across the channel cannot be told as this part of the city is shut off from San Francisco proper.

After darkness, thousands of the homeless were making their way with their blankets and scant provisions to Golden Gate Park and the beach to find shelter. Those in the homes on the hills just north of the Hayes Valley wrecked section piled their belongings in the streets and express wagons and automobiles were hauling the things away to the sparsely settled regions. Everybody in San Francisco is prepared to leave the city, for the belief is firm that San Francisco will be totally destroyed.

Downtown everything is ruin. Not a business house stands. Theatres are crumbled into heaps. Factories and commission houses lie smouldering on their former sites. All of the newspaper plants have been rendered useless. The "Call" and the "Examiner" buildings, excluding the "Call's" editorial rooms on Stevenson street being entirely destroyed.

It is estimated that the loss in San Francisco will reach from $150,000,000 to $300,000,000. These figures are in the rough and nothing can be told until partial accounting is taken.

On every side there was death and suffering yesterday. Hundreds were injured, either burned, crushed or struck by falling pieces from the buildings, and one of ten of the dead will die. The operating table at Mechanics' Pavilion improvised as a hospital for the comfort and care of the injured. The number of dead is not known but it is estimated that at least 500 met their death in the horror.

At nine o'clock, under a special message from President Roosevelt, the city was placed under martial law. Hundreds of troops patrolled the streets and drove the crowds back, while hundreds more were set at work assisting the fire and police departments. The stricken crowds were obedient and bowed to the soldiers' orders during the afternoon three thieves met their death by rifle bullets while at work in the ruins. The guards were ordered back at the breasts of the mobs that the cavalrymen rode and all the crowds were forced from this level district to the hilly section beyond to the north.

The water supply was entirely cut off, and may be it was just as well, for the lines of fire department would have been absolutely useless at any strain. Assistant Chief Dougherty supervised the work of his men and early in the morning it was seen that the only possible chance to save the city lay in effort to check the flames by the use of dynamite. During the day a blast could be heard in any section at intervals of only a few minutes, and buildings not destroyed by fire were blown to atoms. But through the gaps made the flames jumped and although the failures of the heroic efforts of the police firemen and soldiers were at times sickening, the work was continued with a desperation that will live as one of the features of the terrible disaster. Men worked like fiends to combat the laughing, roaring, onrushing fire demon.

Bibliography

BOOKS

Fradkin, Philip L. *The Great Earthquake and Firestorms of 1906*. Berkeley and Los Angeles: University of California Press, 2005.

Kurzman, Dan. *Disaster! The Great San Francisco Earthquake and Fire of 1906*. New York: HarperCollins Publishers, 2001.

Winchester, Simon. *A Crack in the Edge of the World: America and the Great California Earthquake of 1906*. New York: HarperCollins Publishers, 2005.

OTHER PUBLICATIONS

Burke, Emma. Eyewitness account of the San Francisco earthquake of 1906. *Overlook Magazine*. June 2, 1906.

Doyle, Jim. "The Great Quake: 1906-2006 / Horse-drawn hearse leads Santa Rosa quake centennial event." *San Francisco Chronicle*. April 18, 2006.

"The Dire Calamity and the Greater San Francisco." *Organized Labor*, Official Organ of the State and Local Building Trades Councils of California, San Francisco (no byline). April 21, 28 and May 5, 1906 combined edition.

"HUNDREDS DEAD!" *San Francisco Daily News* (no byline). April 18, 1906.

Made in the USA
Middletown, DE
21 September 2022